Venice

115 • COLOUR ILLUSTRATIONS • 1 MAP

St. Mark's Basin. Sunset.

Cover:
Rialto Bridge.

STORTI  EDIZIONI

Scuola Grande di San Rocco. Façade.

Church of Santa Maria dei Frari.

Accademia Galleries. V. Carpaccio, the Legend
of St.Ursula. (Det.).

Ca' D'Oro.
Façade.

Church of the Salute.

Basilica of SS. Giovanni and Paolo.

Rialto Bridge.

St. Mark's Basin.

St. Mark's Square, Basilica and Bell-Tower.

San Giorgio.

The origins of Venice. During the long course of a historical process that had begun when the Roman Empire showed the first signs of an impeding decadence, the Tenth Region, that is Venetia et Histria, was one of the areas most tortured. Life within the region became ever more precarious as the years

Aerial View of the island of S. Francesco del Deserto.

went by. The population learned to its cost the wisdom of abandoning property, dragging away what goods they could, to seek refuge in the Lagoon isles. The city of Venice, therefore, rose upon the islands of Rivoaltus in the year 810, when a group of men, at the head of whom was Angelo Partecipazio, decided to abandon Malamocco, at that time the most important centre, and to move over to these new islands in the middle of

the lagoon. The new generations thought of their existence in terms of this environment.

Venice. The city offers the visitor ruins, often remains of the 8th, 9th and 10th, centuries built one on top of the other, at Torcello for example, or Murano, or encapsulated in buildings in Venice itself. These are what remains to us of the people who fled the mainland in the time of Attila and the Longobards and took their remote Veneto traditions with them into the waters of the lagoon. Then there is the indelible imprint of Byzantine man, visible in prints of the former Ducal Palace or in the Byzantine archways still to be seen in the city, sometimes still in situ in the archetypal «fondaco-house»

(P. 4-5) Rialto Bridge.

Marciana National Library, Venice. The first residential settlements at Rialto. 16th-century paper codices.

St. Mark's Basin, night view.

sometimes in the original stone- and brick-work of the Basilica of St. Mark's or in the same church's earliest mosaic decorations or in traces to be glimpsed in other churches. And then Gothic man identifiable in the art of the period and its economic development as if recognizing himself as the unopposed dominator of the world: the Ducal Palace, the decoration of St. Mark's, the Ca' d'Oro and many other palaces which still kept within «reasonable» proportions and which clearly betrayed the pervasive oriental influence in its architectural and sculptural decorativism. And Renaissance man, recognizable in St. Mark's Square, in the Piazzetta and the palaces which line the Grand Canal, buildings and spaces in which order, impressiveness and size

Ca' d'Oro. Façade. (Det.).

interrupt the airy, fantastic equilibrium of the city, buildings in which man bursts outside the limits set by the water and declares an affinity with a different tradition, the tradition of Rome which he had so far dominated. The Venetian of the eighteenth century did not make history; nor did he suffer it, living isolated his lagoon city in the water; he meets his peers at the theatre, in the gaming houses in the narrow streets and squares and lets the revolutions flow over his head - both the industrial revolution and the political changes of the century. The discoveries, the struggles of a man destined to dominate the world as was the case with the Veneti of fifteen centuries earlier; now, certainly, with different parameters, though just as human.

ST. MARK'S SQUARE

St. Mark's Square in Venice was constructed by the Serenissima Republic over the course of several centuries: at the beginning, in the 12th century, it was simply the space in front of the Basilica, but in subsequent centuries it was conceived of more as a space to be used for events of a religious and political nature.

The decision to build a private chapel for the Doge, which is in fact what St. Mark's Basilica is, brought about the origin of the square and indeed conditioned its development over the years just as it imposed a dual religious and political character on both the church and the space and buildings around. Thus, from the beginning, the Basilica of St. Mark, which merges into the Doge's Palace on its northern side, stood as the natural fulcrum and point of reference for the architecture of the square. This dual character arises out of the functions of the Doge himself, the head of the Venetian state: functions which, despite changes over the centuries, never grew fewer, as evidenced for example by his inalienable right to nominate the chaplain of the Doge's Chapel. Thus the shape of St. Mark's Square, its dimensions and those of the buildings around its perimeter, derived directly from the Basilica: as the church grew, so did the square and the rounded arch of the central archway, which was al-

St. Mark's Square.

St. Mark's Square looking West.

St. Mark's Square looking East.

ready a feature of the façade in the 12th century, was adopted throughout the buildings around the Square. The religious function of the Square as a continuation of the church immediately becomes evident if one observes the façade of the Basilica. It is extremely rich in overtly religious imagery and serves not only to prepare the observer for the interior but also as a great altar for the common people who were admitted into the Basilica only on certain occasions and had usually to attend services outside in the square.

St. Mark's Square. Tourists relaxing at Café Florian.

Piazzetta San Marco. (Det.).

St. Mark's Square. The Clock Tower.

Piazzetta San Marco. Views.

ST. MARK'S BASILICA

In the year 832 the first church was dedicated to St. Mark the Evangelist whose remains, legend has it, were stolen from a monastery in Alexandria in Egypt by two Venetian sailors, and brought to Venice. The Evangelist's symbol, the winged lion, was adopted as the symbol of the city, with St. Mark as its patron saint. The church, called the Church of the Partecipazio because built by Angelo Partecipazio, whose family gave the city seven doges between 811 and 939, was destroyed in 976 when the populace set fire to the Ducal Palace during an uprising, to take doge Pietro IV Candiano. The next doge, Pietro Orseolo, began the restoration and rebuilding of the ruined buildings. In 1063, while Pietro Contarini was doge, work began for the rebuilding of the Basilica, and at his death in 1071 the basic fabric of the basilica was completed; its consecration, occurring in 1094. This is the church we see today but with constant successive embellishments, decoration, marble and mosaic facings. The finishing of the basilica was completed in the 15th century with the superb luxuriant foliage motif of the crowning.

St. Mark's Square. St. Mark's Basilica .

St. Mark's Lion.

The mosaic above St. Alipio's Portal is particularly interesting for the evidence it offers of the contemporary façade of the Basilica and also of the mosaic depicting Christ. The façade of the Basilica as seen in the mosaic is surmounted by three domes. The façade is divided horizontally into two, the lower section with five portals and the upper part rising to the great arches. The dividing line is the loggia on which stand the four gilded horses. These noble beasts give an impression of great agility and movement, as if they were running. The horses of St. Mark's express a sense of unlimited freedom and energy. The façade is dominated by the great mosaic figure of Christ with the Book of the Law. The figures in the mosaic are arranged in seven groups around the front of the façade as the body of St. Mark is taken into the Basilica. Two prelates with their pastoral staffs bear the casket on their shoulders and enter the main doorway while the Doge and other government dignitaries are

St. Mark's Basilica. Main Portal.

St. Mark's Basilica. Main Façade. Sant'Alipio's Portal.

grouped around the doorways on the right. From the portals on the left other dignitaries are coming out to meet their saint, and yet further groups, less involved in the proceedings, stand to right and left. Both the onlookers and the basilica itself are surrounded by so much gold that the atmosphere does pretend to reflect reality; indeed the gold and the schematic nature of the representation seem to confer a metaphysical aura. The church, the

St. Mark's Basilica. The Four Horses.

centre of religion, and the Doge, the symbol of power, are both presented in this illustration as being outside the reality of every day. At the time this mosaic was completed fifty years had passed since Venice conquered Constantinople. The city was overflowing with Byzantine artists many of whom must have collaborated on this mosaic in which religion and politics are represented as being outside

any question of discussion: they were both simply accepted. These horses, transported from the hippodrome of Constantinople by the Venetians in 1204 after the Venetian conquest during the Fourth Crusade, remain an enigma as to the date of their casting, the composition of the metal alloy, and their place of origin. Various hypotheses have been put forward, Greece and Rome, bronze and copper, 4th century B.C. and 2nd century A.D. etc., but still nothing can be said with certainty despite all efforts. What is certain, however, is their importance to the Venetian state over the centuries as a symbol of force and power. It was to neutralise this power among other reasons, that Napoleon had them carried off to Paris after his conquest of Venice. On their return to the city during the Austrian regime the horses were reinstated on the Basilica.

The four Horses in the Marciana Museum.

St. Mark's Basilica. West Façade. Upper Section.　　　　　　　*St. Mark's Basilica. Gothic Crowning (Det.).*

The **four large lunettes** of the upper part of the main façade of the Basilica are decorated with 17th century mosaics executed by A. Gaetano to cartoons by Maffio Verona of scenes from the Life of Christ. The most moving effect of these mosaics is the reflection of the light of the setting sun (the façade faces west) when they seem to come alive in a glory of dazzling colour and light. This effect may be seen, even from the Piazza, during late spring and summer afternoons. Towards the end of the 14th century the construction of the magnificent Gothic crowning motif of foliage and aedicules above the large lunettes was begun. Work was started under the direction of the Delle Masegne and continued later by numerous master sculptors, many of them Tuscan.

In fact Tuscan artists were probably responsible for the majority of the decorations of the niches and statuary. Particularly important are the names of Niccolò Lamberti and his son Pietro, together with artists from his workshop.

This was towards the beginning of the 15th century, when Humanist art was rapidly gaining ascendancy in Florence.

The **interior** of the basilica rests on a platform raised considerably above the level of the Piazza according to antique custom in the building of temples and basilicas, to stress the sanctity of the place. It has a Greek cross floorplan, of limited dimensions yet at the same time difficult to read or define. The flooring is in marble mosaic, the columns of rare marbles, the

St. Mark's Basilica
Floor Mosaic. (Det.).

walls lined with slabs of marble in various colours below, and with mosaics in glass and gold above, as are the cupolas. One has the impression of walking over a rich Oriental carpet in various designs, surrounded by a half-light which accentuates the gleaming richness of the golden mosaics of the upper parts. The mosaics and their reflections seem to dissolve the contours of the arches and cupolas, multiplying the space. This is a profoundly religious building, once the chapel of the doges of Venice, and its origins are bound up in the history of this city poised between East and West, for centuries the all-powerful, greatly feared mistress of the Adriatic, of which it is the most potent symbol. It is Byzantine in its floorplan, its arches, cupolas, decoration and sense of opulence; Romanesque in its structure. Two worlds meet and combine to create a new, unique and inimitable masterpiece.

St. Mark's Basilica. Narthex.

St. Mark's Basilica. Rood Screen. (Det.).

St. Mark's Basilica. Central Nave and Presbytery.

St. Mark's Basilica. South Transept and Gothic Rose Window.

St. Mark's Basilica . Presbytery and Main Altar.

St. Mark's Basilica. Presbytery, Ciborium and Pala d'Oro.

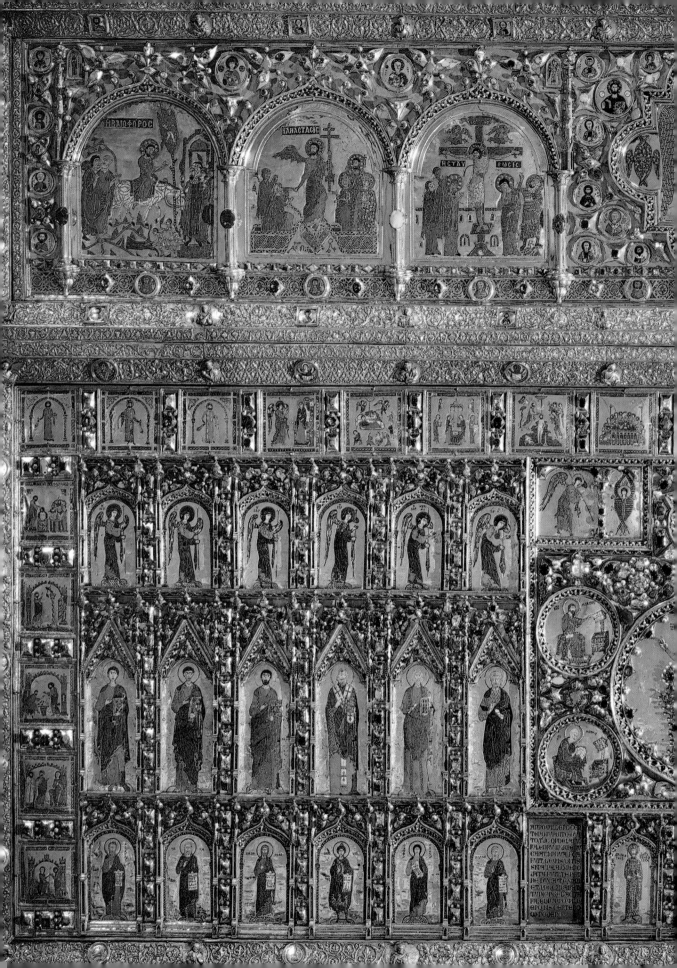

VM MODO REX ORAT SVPPLEX SVA TVRBA SOPORAT ; AD QVOS MOX TENDITE

(P.22-23) St. Mark's Basilica. Pala d'Oro.

St. Mark's Basilica. Right aisle, back wall. Prayer in the Garden (Det.).

(P. 24) St. Mark's Basilica, Pala d'Oro. The Pantocrator.

St. Mark's Basilica. The large Arches of the Ascension Dome.

Space was taken for the **Baptistery** from the south end of the transept in the 14th century and even though it appears as a separate entity, it forms an essential and integral part of the church. It is between the Zen Chapel and the rooms housing the Treasury, on one side of the Piazzetta. The decoration of its interior was executed at intervals over a period of two centuries, the 15th and 16th. It was begun originally by Doge Andrea Dandolo, whose funeral monument, in the form of a hanging urn, is against the wall opposite the entrance (14th cent.). During his term of office the Baptistery was organ-

St. Mark's Basilica. Baptistery. St. Mark.

ised as we still see it today and the mosaics which decorate the vaults and cupolas were executed. Previous to this the wall decorations, which seem to have dated to the 10th century, were frescoed. These mosaics, narrating episodes from the Life of Christ and the Life of John the Baptist, belong to the stream of popular Venetian art and are characterised by great expressive power as seen in the Baptism of Christ, and by certain Gothic traits - the ordering of the figures, the stylized representation of landscape, and the expressions of the faces. The Dance of Salome is the most typical and pure example of the style.

St. Mark's Basilica. Baptistery. The Magi on their way to Bethlehem.

St. Mark's Basilica. Baptistery. Baptismal Basin.

St. Mark's Basilica. Baptistery. The Dance of Salome.

DUCAL PALACE

The **Ducal Palace** was begun in the second decade of the 9th century and the Republic of Venice spared no expense in embellishing both interior and exterior so as to present a fitting symbol of the ideal state. At first it resembled a castle and was primarily built for defensive purposes, assuming in Byzantine and particularly in Gothic times, more open architectural forms. The present building retains the Gothic forms of the 14th century, with wide, open loggias and windows which, together with the precious marble inlay covering of the walls, clearly demonstrate the security and wealth attained by the Venetian state.

Ducal Palace.
The façade on the Piazzetta
as seen from the Loggetta.

Ducal Palace.
The façade on the Piazzetta. (Det.).

Ducal Palace along the Piazzetta. (Det.).

façades. A continuous arcade with 38 sturdy columns surmounted by precious capitals opens onto the Piazzetta and the waterside. On the capitals, and in particular on those at the corners, are sculpted scenes stressing the role of the palace and of the state: symbols of commerce, of war and peace, while the marble group nearest the Porta della Carta depicts the "Judgement of Solomon", embodying the principle of Justice. The artistic level of several of the capitals has led to their being replaced "in situ" by copies, the originals being preserved inside the Museo dell'Opera. Two arches on the upper floor correspond with each arch on the ground floor; each trilobate arch is surmounted by full and intersecting tracery circles forming a motif of crosses within the circles. The walls which spring from this base attain an effect of weightlessness thanks to the coloured marbles arranged to form a rhomboid motif, or open into large windows. From the large cornice above rise alternate white and pink pinnacles, each surmounted by drops of marble. The overall impression is of exotic, orientalising taste.

The Ducal Palace had certain well-defined functions. The section overlooking the canal comprised the Doge's apartment, with the following rooms dedicated to various Venetian magistracies such as the College and the Senate; further on were the Palace of Justice with various courts and the prisons, the "Pozzi" (wells) and the dreaded "Piombi" (literally, leads i.e. under the lead roof) and in the corner near the Ponte della Paglia, the Armoury. In the wing overlooking the Basin is the vast Great Council Hall, and in the wing overlooking the Piazzetta the Hall of Scrutiny. The Palace has a delicate, weightless quality, rather like lace, thanks to its softly coloured design motif, its pinnacles and aedicules. From the photographs on these two pages one can clearly discern the very open character of the architectural forms and the enormously rich decoration of its

Ducal Palace, façade on the Piazzetta. The Statue of Justice.

Ducal Palace, South-west corner. A sculpture with Adam and Eve.

Ducal Palace, west corner, sculpture with the judgement of Salomon.

The Ducal Palace as seen from the island of San Giorgio.

Ducal Palace. The Porta della Carta.

Ducal Palace. The courtyard façade in Renaissance style.

Ducal Palace. The Giants' Staircase.

Ducal Palace. The Golden Staircase.

Ducal Palace. Hall of the Four Doors. G. Caliari, The doge Marino Grimani receives the gifts of the Persian Ambassadors.

Ducal Palace. Hall of the Antecollege. P. Veronese. The Rape of Europa.

Hall of the Four Doors. The function of this hall, as a waiting and "clearing" room, is admirably expressed by the four doors placed symmetrically in the long walls. The hall is in the Palladian style and dates to the second half of the 16th century. The richly decorated stuccoed ceiling panels, by Giovanni Cambi and Maestro Baldissera, frame frescoes by Tintoretto depicting Venetian power.

The **Hall of the Antecollege** was used as an anteroom for the various embassies and delegations waiting for audience with the Signoria. The decorations on the walls, the chimneypiece, the frieze and the vaulted ceiling, with stuccoes, statues, columns, frescoes and mosaics with classical and mythological motifs, form a harmonious and united whole.

On the walls are several well known and prestigious canvases: Jacopo Tintoretto's "Vulcan's Forge", "Mercury and the Graces", "Pallas banishing Mars" and "The Discovery of Ariadne". These allegorical and mythological paintings, executed about 1577, are considered amongst the painter's finest works. Here too are Paolo Veronese's "Rape of Europa" and Jacopo Bassano's "Jacob's Return from Canaan".

Ducal Palace. Hall of the Antecollege.

Ducal Palace. Hall of the Antecollege. J. Tintoretto, Mercury and the Graces.

Ducal Palace. Hall of the College.

Ducal Palace. Hall of the Antecollege. J. Tintoretto, The Discovery of Ariadne.

Hall of the College. The magistrates who formed the College were responsible for the preparation and preliminary discussion of matters to be put to the Senate, dealings with the Roman Church and part of the judiciary power of the state, and for the reception of foreign embassies. The hall was decorated after the fire of 1574 by Palladio and G.A. Rusconi. The intaglio and gilded wooden ceiling executed by F. Bello and

A. Faentin in 1577-78 contains paintings by Veronese, amongst which "Mars and Neptune", "Faith", "Justice and Peace render homage to Venice" and, amongst the symbolic figures, "Fidelity", "Prosperity", "Dialectic", "Meekness". On the walls are paintings by Jacopo Tintoretto, including "The Mystic Marriage of St. Catherine".

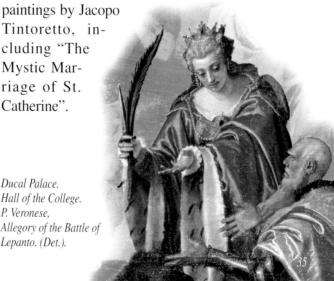

Ducal Palace. Hall of the College. P. Veronese, Allegory of the Battle of Lepanto. (Det.).

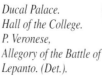

35

REIPVB
FVNDAMEN
TVM

CVSTO
DES LIBER
TATIS.

Ducal Palace.
Hall of the College.
The Ceiling. (Det.).

Ducal Palace. Hall of the College.
P. Veronese, Dialectic.

Ducal Palace. Hall of the College.
Ceiling. Faith, the Strength of the Republic.

Ducal Palace. Hall of the College. Ceiling.
P. Veronese, Justice and Peace.

Ducal Palace. Senate Hall.

Ducal Palace. Senate Hall. Ceiling. (Det.).

Senate Hall. The magistracy of the Senate was one of the most important in the Republic. Constituted in 1229, its members were limited in the 14th century to sixty, to which in later centuries were added the "Zonte", commissions comprising a variable number of patricians. This assembly deliberated all the political actions of the Republic, in particular decisions to declare war, the nomination of magistrates, the Patriarch and the Bishops, and study commissions to draft new laws and reforms in the various state departments. In Venice the members of the Senate were also known as the "Pregadi" because the Doge "prayed" them to enter the Senate Hall from the Hall of the Four Doors, where they were waiting, at the beginning of each session. The room was decorated between 1580 and 1595. The ceiling, with its great panels and richly scrolled and gilded frames, was executed by Cristoforo Sorte around 1581. The paintings date to 1585-95, when Pasquale Cicogna was Doge, and include "Doge Venier and the subject cities" by J. Palma the Younger.

The Council of Ten founded the **Armoury** in the 16th century to defend the state after ongoing revolts, some even breaching the Doge's Palace itself. The original arms were added to over time by others left to the State by patrician families; gifts from visiting dignitaries and ambassadors; or entire collections of arms left by famous soldiers. The collection comprises odd pieces including a pennon a bronze culverin, an arquebus as well as assorted swords, pikes, harquebuses and musketoons.

Ducal Palace. Armoury, Morosini Hall

Ducal Palace. A cell called "Pozzi".

Ducal Palace, New Prisons. A cell.

Ducal Palace. Senate Hall. Ceiling. J. Tintoretto, The Triumph of Venice.

Great Council Hall. This is the largest hall in the palace, measuring 54 x 25 x 12 metres. The Great Council was the greatest magistracy in the state and from the time of its inception on, it increased in numbers from three hundred to one thousand six hundred.

The decoration of the hall which we see today dates to 1578-95 and was effected by numerous artists, including Tintoretto, Paolo Veronese and Jacopo Palma the Younger.

Ducal Palace.
Hall of the Great Council.
J. Tintoretto, "Paradise" (Det.).

Ducal Palace.
Hall of the Great Council.

The canvases depict the most important episodes in the history of Venice.

The Bridge of Sighs. The bridge is a suspended passageway between the Doge's Palace and Prisons. The Prisons' walls are made of crudely finished massive blocks of stone, the windows are narrow and barred, and the doors are equipped with chains and bolts. The building reminds us of the legendary escape of Casanova.

Bridge of Sighs.

St' Mark's Basin and Grand Canal

St. Mark's Basin is that expanse of water in front of the Molo (quay) of San Marco, with San Giorgio facing the island of Giudecca to the right; nearer to the right is the Punta della Dogana with the adjacent church of the Salute. San Giorgio, the Dogana (customs house) and the Salute may be considered three pearls ornamenting the entrance into Venice, the Quay. Our excursion along the Grand Canal begins here, and the gondolier will carry us gently up as far as the station and Piazzale Roma. Should we be fortunate enough to set out at sunset during the summer months, with that particular light and the water, the city would offer an unforgettable experience.

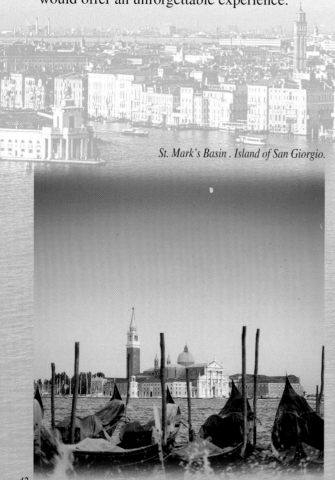

St. Mark's Basin . Island of San Giorgio.

St. Mark's Basin. Island of San Giorgio.

St. Mark's Basin, Dogana da Mar.

St. Mark's Basin. Dogana da Mar and church of the Salute.

St. Mark's Basin. Aerial View.
(P. 46-47) Sunset over the Grand Canal.

The **area** stretching from the Salute to the Academy on one side, and as far as the quays of the Zattere on the other, is one of the most picturesque in the city, well worth a visit.

There are small squares with fine well-heads overlooked, for example, by the façade of a Gothic church (Campo San Gregorio); narrow "calli" (Venetian for street) leading into wider "salizzade"; picturesque canals, and people talking, walking, stopping to look while a delicious smell of fried fish wafts out from the houses which are generally low, often single-storeyed.

Grand Canal. Dario Palace.

View of the Grand Canal and the Lagoon
Grand Canal. Barbarigo Palace with the Façade decorated with mosaics.

Grand Canal. Grassi Palace.

Accademia Galleries. Vittore Carpaccio, the Legend of St.Ursula.

Accademia Galleries. Vittore Carpaccio, The Legend of St. Ursula.

Accademia Galleries. Gentile Bellini, Miracle of the Cross at S. Lorenzo.

Grand Canal. Ca' Rezzonico.

Ca' Rezzonico. F. Guardi, the Nuns' Parlour.   *Ca' Rezzonico. The Ballroom.*

Cà Da Mosto, is one of the oldest and best preserved buildings in the city. The ground and first floors are typical of 13th century Veneto-Byzantine architecture, with high narrow arches, characteristic capitals and the open nature of the upper floor. The dwelling-cum-warehouse has remained intact, on the exterior at least, even in its decorative roundels and panels. The upper section was added in the 17th century. The name derives from the fact that the great seaman Alvise Da Mosto was born in the palace in 1432, and the early architectural forms indicate that the area was inhabited from ancient times.

(P. 54-55) Rialto Bridge. The Historic Regata.

Grand Canal. Ca' da Mosto.

Grand Canal. Ca' Pesaro, Museum of Modern Art.
Vittorio Zecchin, A Thousand and One Nights.

Grand Canal. Ca' Pesaro, Museum of Modern Art.
The Grand Canal at Ca' d'Oro.

Grand Canal. Ca' d'Oro, façade. (Det.).

The **Church of the Frari** is an architectural element of the former monastic complex comprising two cloisters, the cells of the Franciscan monks and rooms for meetings and prayer. The complex as we see it today dates to the 14th, 15th and 16th centuries. The church is now visited by a large number of people, both for its architectural interest, in that its Gothic forms are punctuated by wide rhythms in both a horizontal and a vertical sense, and for its rich patrimony of works of art. Foremost among them are Titian's Assumption of the Virgin and the Pesaro Madonna, Giovanni Bellini's exquisite triptych, Donatello's St. John the Baptist, a triptych by Bartolomeo Vivarini, the Monument to Doge Tron by Antonio Rizzo and a statue of John the Baptist by Sansovino.

Church of the Frari. Main Altar..
Tiziano Vecellio, Assumption. (Det.).

Church of the Frari.

Campo SS. Giovanni e Paolo. The School, the Basilica, the monument.　　*Andrea Verrocchio. Equestrian Statue of Bartolomeo Colleoni.*

SS. Giovanni e Paolo is the name of a noted monastic complex of the Dominican order, at the north-east of the city. The complex comprised the church, cloisters, gardens and meeting and prayer rooms. The Dominicans today perform services in the church, and the cloisters, gardens and conventual buildings have been given over to the city hospital, together with the buildings of the former Scuola di San Marco, adjacent to the church. Since the 13th century, when the order received land to build on in the area from Doge Jacopo Tiepolo, SS. Giovanni e Paolo increased continually in importance and prestige. The church early became a burial-place for many Doges and was enriched with prestigious works of art and funeral monuments, and as in many other parts of Italy and Europe became the "opposite number" of the Franciscan church of the Frari. The view from the square outside already provides a strong sense of beauty and majesty, with the simple pedestal of the extremely powerful figure of the mercenary general, Colleoni exemplifying courage and strength; the façade of the Scuola di San Marco with its sculptures and beautiful marbles, provides a note of refined elegance. The interior of the church repeats the movement of the Frari church, but is lighter thanks to the southern orientation of the apse.

The most noteworthy works of art include a polyptych by G. Bellini, canvases by G.B. Piazzetta and P. Veronese, and the numerous funeral monuments ranged along the walls.

We have thus arrived at so-called **"Minor Venice"**, lesser known but not for this less original and interesting, and perhaps more "immediate", tangible. This Venice offers unusual spatial solutions, such as these bridges with the salizzada, i.e., a small street along a canal. The Contarini Palace has those marble strips connecting its balconies in widespread use throughout the city as decorative elements. In the Querini Stampalia Palace is to be found a picture gallery that contains a rich collection of paintings including a "Presentation in the Temple" by Giovanni Bellini and a "Judith" by V. Catena, as well as the exquisite "Duck Hunt in the Lagoon" by P. Longhi.

Contarini dal Bovolo Palace.

The canal and bridge of S.Andrea.

The **Theatre** enjoyed enormous popularity in Venice particularly during the 17th and 18th centuries, and there were numerous theatrical establishments sponsored by wealthy noblemen throughout the city. The Teatro **La Fenice** was built shortly before the fall of the Republic and its large auditorium reflected pure Baroque taste. This building was burnt down and in 1832 the Meduna brothers constructed the present building, retaining the Baroque decorative scheme of the auditorium but designing the other rooms in the Neoclassical style. In the year 1996 the Theater was destroyed another time by fire and at present is being rebuilt.

San Giovanni Crisostomo. Corte del Milion.

The Interior of the La Fenice Theatre .

MURANO AND BURANO

Amongst the islands of the lagoon, many of which have disappeared over the centuries while others have emerged and formed, **Murano** is one of the most famous. This fame is to a large degree due to the traditional production of glass there, which is known as Murano glass. The historical origins of this production on Murano are not known; in the beginning it appears that glass was produced in Venice itself, but a state decree ordered the removal of the furnaces to Murano because of the number of fires they had caused in the city. This occurred from the 12th to the 13th century, but Murano had already served as a place of refuge for fugi-

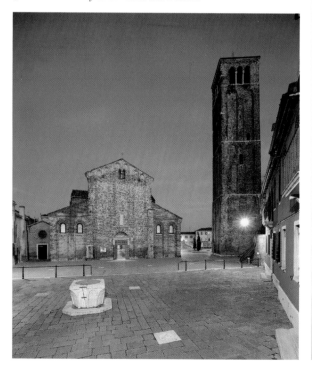

Murano glass.

Murano. Basilica of Santa Maria and Donato.

Burano. View.

tives from the mainland and in later centuries the Venetian nobility built villas, monasteries and churches on the island.

The island of **Burano** has made no distinctive mark on the history of the people of the lagoon; it has neither ancient traditions nor noteworthy monuments.

It is thus to be presumed that for centuries it remained a hamlet of fishermen and others connected with the sea, and in fact it is still basically a fishing village. But another activity has proved singularly important: lacemaking, with which the women would occupy themselves as they awaited the return of their menfolk. Burano should be visited with this important fact in mind, to fully appreciate the small houses, the cadence of the dialect, the perfect union of water, man and environment.

Torcello is an island very close to Burano, but it remains, solitary and humble as it appears today, one of the most important centres of the origin of the Venetian state. Its importance for the fugitives from the mainland seeking some place offering sufficient security for settlement, was dictated by its position in respect to the mainland. The fugitives who settled here came from Altino, fleeing before the Longobard hordes, and brought with them the sacred remains of their patron saint from their abandoned city, naming it Torcello from the Tower (Italian "torre"), symbol of their lost homeland. They also brought with them their habits and customs, their language and their laws and the entire social structure which had regulated their lives together until that moment. And lastly they brought an artistic tradition, of classical origins. On Torcello they built a house of God and a Baptistery, and their own houses clustered around them, rude and poor certainly in the beginning, but increasingly grand as they began to trade and do business, to organise a new kind of life in the middle of the water.

The visitor to Torcello is immediately struck by the whole environment -water, mudflats, flights of birds, solitude- and by the extreme nobility of the 11th century campanile, despite its simplicity, and of the 11th century cathedral of S. Maria Assunta and the 11th-12th century church of S. Fosca. In front of the cathedral are the remains of the 7th century Baptistery; inside, a superb mosaic covering the end wall and dignified architectural forms, and a powerful mosaic of the Virgin at once mystical, ethereal, metaphysical.

Torcello. Church of Santa Fosca.

Venice

CONTENTS

Graphics: Storti Edizioni S.r.l.

Photography:
Storti Archive
Cameraphoto**arte** Venezia
SIME

Text: Storti Editorial Staff

STORTI EDIZIONI S.r.l.

Via Brianza, 9/C - 30030 Oriago di Mira (VE)
TEL. 041.5659057 - 041.5659058
FAX 041.5631157
INTERNET: www.stortiedizioni.it
e-mail: edstort@tin.it

Cover:
St. Mark's Basilica. Façade.